Contents

Tackle for stillwater fly fishing

When choosing tackle it is necessary to consider whether it is for bank or boat fishing. If it is bank fishing, further consider the style of fishing—orthodox wet fly, nymph fishing or long-range wet fly and lure fishing with a shooting head—and then choose the tackle which will be most effective for it.

How then do you go about selecting the rod which will be most suitable for your type of stillwater fishing? First it is necessary to consider rod action, length and the line weight best suited to a particular action.

Figure A shows a tip-action rod and figure B a butt-action rod. The shaded area is the part which flexes when the rod is in use. It can be seen that the shaded area in A is much smaller than in B. The energy is concentrated towards the tip in A and provides a much quicker acceleration which transmits the energy to the line and gives it the greater speed which is essential for distance. When the rod tip travels only a short distance a narrow arc is formed and, hence, a narrow line loop. If the rod travels a long distance a wide arc (and wide line loop) is formed. A narrow line loop is much better for accuracy and distance since there is a smaller area to be affected by wind and air resistance.

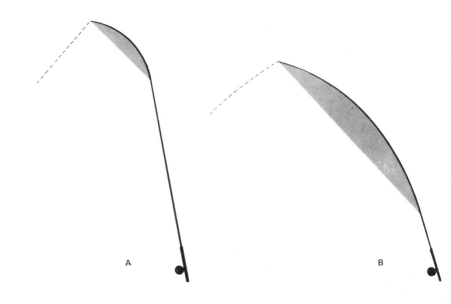

A   B

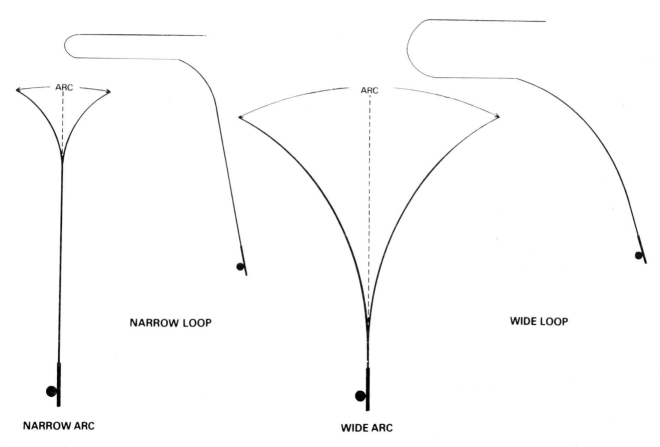

ARC

NARROW LOOP

ARC

WIDE LOOP

NARROW ARC

WIDE ARC

Let us now consider the three basic actions for a trout fly rod: (1) slow or soft action, (2) medium action and (3) fast or tip action. Photograph 1 shows a slow action; note that the casting curve is from the rod tip right down to the casting hand. This type of action is best with light lines (AFTM 3 to 5) where distance is not required. If a heavy line is used it overloads the rod and kills its action.

Photograph 2 shows mid- (or three-quarter) action. A medium-action rod is very good for orthodox wet fly and nymph fishing when light leaders call for a light strike. With this kind of rod you will need AFTM 5–6 fly lines.

Photograph 3 shows the action of a fast or tip-action rod. This kind of rod will impart greater tip speed to the line to cast faster and further. These rods are best with shooting-head and forward-tapered lines. It is essential to use the correct line weight—normally AFTM7, 8 or 9.

Rod length is also very important. Many people make the mistake of thinking that the longer the rod, the greater the distance that can be cast but they forget that a long rod can be

Slow action.

Medium action.

4

very tiring since it exerts more leverage against the caster with a resulting loss of accuracy and finesse. For reservoir bank fishing I prefer a carbon or boron rod of 9 ft 6 ins. (The J.T. Champion rod, which I designed and which is available from Marcus Warwick, 58 High Street West, Uppingham, Rutland 9QD, is ideal for 8 and 9 double-tapered lines and shooting heads.) I use a long rod only when boat fishing on reservoirs—a light 11 ft boron rod which is useful for working the bob-fly.

As for lines—it is the weight of fly line to be cast which determines the rod action which can best propel a particular weight. Many anglers forget that a flyline is basically an elongated weight. The AFTM line system is based on the weight of the first 30 ft of line, which, when aerialised, flexes the rod properly. The higher the line number, the heavier the line. However, rods can handle different line weights and this is done by increasing the line weight by lengthening or shortening the line in order to get the correct length which flexes the rod properly. A rod which has an AFTM 7 rating can be used with a No. 6 line simply by having more line

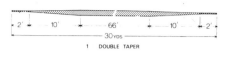

1 DOUBLE TAPER

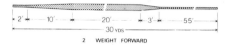

2 WEIGHT FORWARD

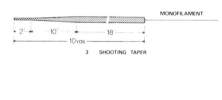

3 SHOOTING TAPER

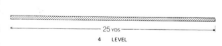

4 LEVEL

st action.

which will increase the weight in the air. Always think in terms of the flyline as an elongated weight and this should help you to understand the relationship between the line and the rod.

Basically there are three types of line for stillwater fishing—(1) double taper, (2) forward taper and (3) shooting head. A fourth type, the level line, can be very useful for boat fishing.

Double-tapered lines are probably the most popular lines for orthodox wet fly and nymph fishing on reservoirs. The advantage of the double-tapered line is that it can be picked up quickly off the water, and this is of particular use when a quick change of direction is required. Double-tapered lines are easier to retrieve, particularly by the figure-of-eight technique. Another advantage of double-taper lines is that when one taper starts to wear it is just a matter of reversing the line on the reel and you virtually have a new line. It pays to buy a good double-tapered line—properly cared for it will give several years of use.

Forward-tapered lines are designed for distance casting. They are constructed with a heavy front section followed by a much thinner line which shoots easily. These lines are good for casting into the wind and for distance; also, compared with monofilament, the thin shooting line is fairly easily retrieved.

Shooting heads attached to monofilament are the lines to use for maximum distance. the 'heads' can be attached to other thin shooting lines e.g. braided nylon, dacron or thin backing line, which are all easier to handle than monofilament.

Once you have mastered distance casting it is up to you to find the shooting head which you feel you can handle with ease. There are several methods of attaching them to monofilament and other lines, but I find the following to be as good as any.

I prefer Fuji or silicon carbide rings throughout, with the butt ring being a two-legged Fuji and the intermediate rings single-legged. My experiments with various rod rings have convinced me that Fuji and silicon carbide rings give more distance.

The reel should be as light as possible. A heavy reel is more weight in the hand which has to be moved every time a cast is made. Heavy rods and reels lead to fatigue and impaired performance.

The knot I use for attaching tournament and stillwater shooting heads has never let me down. This knot can be made very quickly. Pass the monofilament four times over the end of the fly line as shown in the sketch and then insert the end of the monofilament through the formed loops and pull both ends of the mono tight. Varnish the join.

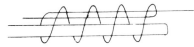

Casting fundamentals

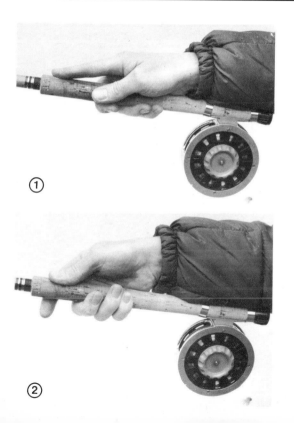

It is often the simplest points which present a great deal of trouble—an example being the wrong way of holding a rod. The rod grip is very important, particularly in stillwater fishing where long casting is often required. Photograph 1 shows the index finger extended along the handle, the grip often used by newcomers to stillwater fly fishing. Using this grip when casting on stillwaters results not only in straining the finger but also in restricting the back cast movement.

The thumb along the top of the handle in Photograph 2 is much better and often used, particularly for long back casts.

It is best, however, to use the grip shown in Photograph 3 with the thumb angled to the left; this is a much more relaxed grip and allows freer movement of the wrist.

Once you are satisfied with your grip, put on the line, leader and reel and lay out some 40 ft of line in front of you and hold the line as shown on the right. Get into the habit of keeping tension on the section of line between the butt ring and free hand in both back and forward casts.

Before making any rod movement let us consider the position of feet and legs, for these play an important part. For a right-handed caster the feet should be angled to the right and be about 21 in. apart for normal casting, but for longer casts, as will be explained in the section on the double haul, the stance is wider. Angling the feet to the right makes it easier to watch the line in the back cast, and the proper width of stance gives good body weight distribution.

Shooting line: in order to achieve distance in the forward cast, strip a few yards of line from the reel and leave in loose coils at your feet. As the rod reaches the ten o'clock position in the forward cast, release line with the left hand and the loose coils will shoot out and extend the length of cast.

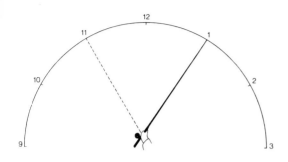

To understand the various casting arcs it helps to visualise a clock face. In normal casting the arc of rod movement is from eleven to one, as shown on the left.

For a high back cast the arc should be tilted forward as shown below left.

For a low back cast the arc should be tilted backward as shown below.

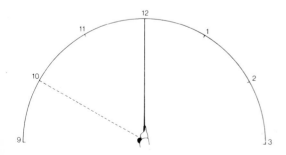

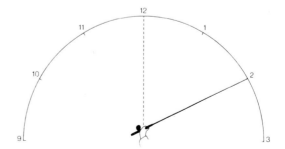

The next set of photographs show various stages in rod positioning for the forward and back cast of the ordinary trout fly cast, which will help to clarify the mechanics of the operation. The rod can be used through a wide or a narrow arc when performing the trout fly cast. Using the rod through a wide arc as shown in Photographs 1 and 2 results in the line forming a wide loop. This wide loop is a great handicap to distance casting on reservoirs as it offers a greater area for air and wind resistance. Accuracy, particularly in the wind, is also impaired because a wide loop has poor line speed and is not so positive in presenting the fly or lure.

Tapered balanced leaders are essential for good fly presentation, proper line turnover and casting into the wind. The butt section of the leader should be practically as thick as the end of the fly line tapering to the point. The size of the fly or lure is important in relation to the leader point. The larger the fly the heavier the point and vice versa. A large fly on a thin point will result in poor control and presentation on the forward cast. Leaders can be constructed by using various thick-

Using the rod through a wide arc.

nesses of monofilament starting from 20 lb breaking strain at the end of the fly line to between 4 and 8 lb at the point of the leader. I prefer to have a permanent 2 ft length of monofilament tied by a nail knot to the end of the fly line. I attach my leaders by means of the simple blood knot to this 2 ft length of monofilament. I also prefer to buy knotless tapered leaders. Most of my fly

fishing on stillwaters is done with an 11 ft leader on which I normally use three flies. However, for nymph and lure fishing I prefer a long 16 ft leader.

For river fishing I use much shorter leaders—between 8 ft and 5 ft 6 ins.

Now look at Photographs 3–5 showing the rod being used on a narrow arc which results in a narrow line loop— much better for distance casting, ac-

curacy and line control. You will also note that the casting arm is moving backward and forward on the same plane. If the planes are separated (which is very common) and the angler starts making a circular motion, the line also follows this circular motion and consequently forms the undesirable wideline loop. Practise until you are casting with a good tight line loop.

The rod being used through a narrow arc.

Several angling writers in the past have advocated keeping the wrist stiff at the completion of the back cast. However, it has been shown that the faster a muscle contracts the less force it is capable of exerting. In relation to casting the more we spread the accelerating forces of the whole arm the more force we are capable of exerting. This can be proved by locking the elbow and moving the upper arm. The hand will move at a given speed. If the elbow is then allowed to open and close the speed of the hand is increased without putting a greater load on the muscles which move the upper arm. Wrist movement will increase the speed of the hand further without increasing the muscle load. It is the final flick of the wrist in the back and forward casts that imparts the greatest amount of tip speed to the line—locking the wrist prevents this.

Now try casting following this sequence: first, pillow the butt of the rod under the forearm (get into the habit of doing this—it gives much greater leverage for the start of the back cast which is particularly useful for long casting on still-waters). The wrist should be turned down and the forearm at the horizontal at the start of the back cast. The forearm is moved vertically toward the head and then the wrist is flicked over at chin level and the movement stopped at just about eye level (Photographs 1–4). The 12 yards of line will end up on the ground behind you. Make sure it is straight since a straight back cast is the basis of a good forward cast.

The back cast: the wrist is flicked over at chin level.

In this photograph sequence the action goes from right to left.

You will see from Photographs 5–8 that the forward cast is the reverse of the back cast—flick the wrist over just before the rod reaches the horizontal and allow the line to drift onto the ground. Aim about four feet above the ground then follow through for good turnover and delicate presentation. If the cast is aimed too near the water instead of a few feet above, the splashy presentation often scares the fish.

Practise these movements, this time with the line in the air, remembering to keep the line between the butt ring and left hand tight in both back and forward casts, and not to separate the planes. Once you feel things are right, go though the same drill on the water. Never practise too long on land as this can lead to a lazy back cast due to there being no surface water tension at the start of the back cast.

When you feel you have mastered the back and forward cast, try varying the arc of rod movement to get a high back cast, which is very useful when there is a dam wall behind and also gives a low forward cast for casting into the wind. Stop the rod movement with the rod at about twelve o'clock.

The forward cast: flick the wrist over just before the rod reaches the horizontal.

For a low back cast, lower the rod on the back cast to two o'clock. This will result in a high forward cast which is desirable for good distance when the wind is behind you. Lowering the back cast when the wind is behind you also results in a tighter line loop and therefore helps to penetrate the wind. Always aim for a good straight back cast.

Common casting faults

A very common fault amongst still-water casters and one which is the most likely to scare fish is a splashy presentation. This is caused by keeping the power on too long in the forward cast through aiming the rod too low at the water.

To cure this fault, imagine a level four feet above the water and try to cast along it, allowing the flies to *drift* on to the water. Another technique for delicate fly presentation is to shoot a little line every time the line straightens out in the forward cast and you will find that the fly and leader land much more gently.

Another common reason for losing a good fish is the appearance of knots in the leader, thus weakening the material leading to a breakage. Knots appearing on the leader can be caused by (1) starting to forward cast before the line has had time to straighten in the back cast (this also results in flies being snapped off); (2) not lowering the power stroke enough when casting into the wind with the result that the leader doubles back on itself and often forms a knot. But probably the most common cause is tipping the rod forward and then pushing forcibly with the casting hand. The rod should be pushed forward only at the end of the forward cast.

Snapping (or whip-cracking) the line in the back cast will lose many flies. It is caused by starting the forward cast too soon before the line has a chance to straighten in the back cast, or not putting sufficient effort into the back cast to ensure the line straightens out.

To correct these faults, watch the back cast and make sure the line straightens out before making the forward cast. Also ensure that sufficient power is put into the back cast to enable the line to straighten. Gradually, however, you will develop the correct 'feel' and know instinctively when the line straightens. Pausing too long in the back cast or taking the rod too far back results in the line and flies catching up on the ground behind you. To avoid this, again get into the habit, when learning, of watching the line straighten in the back cast; when it straightens make the forward cast. Gradually you will be able to time the exact moment for making the forward cast and then it will be no longer necessary to watch the line at the rear.

When learning, remember also not to let the rod drift beyond the one o'clock position, otherwise the line can also end up on the ground. Once your line control becomes more proficient by the correct use of the left hand, however, you will be able to allow the rod to drift well back (particularly in the double haul technique) without the line touching the ground or water in the back cast.

False casting

False casting is where the fly is cast but is not allowed to touch the water. There are occasions when the dry fly can be very successful on reservoirs and it is then essential that the artificial be kept dry in order that it floats properly.

Another use for false casting is to change the direction of the cast without the line touching the water. Often when fishing a loch or reservoir, cruising trout are quickly sucking down flies from the surface. These large fish can change their direction quickly. If a fish is missed but is seen to be rising to flies in a different position, it is a simple matter to change direction by false casting.

A third use is to extend the line in the air before presenting the fly to a rising fish. Line is slipped out gradually with the left hand until the fish can be reached and, since the fly and line do not touch the water until the required moment, there is less chance of scaring the fish.

④ ③ ② ①

Distance casting

It is wise when beginning to learn distance fly casting to tone up the casting muscles. This is particularly important after a long lay-off during the winter months. Casting muscles which are out of condition lead to a tired arm and result in a poor casting technique which exaggerates faults.

The double-haul technique can be learned with several rod actions and line weights. I found that it is worth practising for a time with a tip-action rod and No. 7 double-tapered line and then moving on fairly quickly to a shooting head of 34 ft attached to 20 lb breaking-strain monofilament.

When attempting to learn the double-haul, always get into the habit of keeping the line tight with the left hand and pulling the line down a few inches at the start of every back cast; this increases the line speed and gives control of the back cast. Remember also, when doing the forward cast, not only to keep tension on the line with the left hand to increase line speed but also to give another slight pull on the line. Getting into the habit of making these two small pulls helps greatly in understanding the 'feel' of the double-haul.

The first step is to run off 16 yds of line in front of you and then pull back 5 yds and drop it at your feet, which should be positioned as shown in Photograph 1. For a right-handed caster, the left foot is straight in front and the right foot angled to the right. You should hold the rod firmly but not too tightly—a tight grip strains the hand and affects casting.

①

⑦ ⑥ ⑤ ④

Now to the back cast; with the left hand holding the line near the top of the rod handle, start to make an orthodox casting movement with your right hand, at the same time making a long haul (see Photograph 2) with the left hand. Ideally, the timing of the first haul should coincide with the fastest movement of the rod. This precise timing will come with practice. When you start the haul, turn your head and watch the line movement.

If you look at the photograph you will see that when the cast starts, the body weight is over the left leg and, as the movement progresses to the rear, the body weight is transferred onto the right leg. The line, because it has been hauled, is moving back a lot faster than in normal casting.

As the line loop is turning over in the back cast you will

feel the line which is being held in the left hand being pulled upwards (see Photographs 3 and 4). Don't resist this— allow the left hand to move upwards towards the right (Photographs 5 and 6). You must always remember to maintain tension on the section of line between the left hand and the butt ring. You will also note that the body weight has been transferred to the right leg. Note in Photo-graphs 6 and 7 how the tension is being kept on the line with the left hand. Note that the left hand holding the line has moved almost to the reel. From this position the forward cast begins.

Practise these movements until you have proper control of the line and remember to keep the line under tension throughout.

⑧   ⑨   ⑩   ⑪

When comparing Photographs 2 and 4 you will note that the casting hand has dropped considerably. This has been achieved by transferring the body weight onto a bent right leg and by partially straightening the right arm.

The simplest way to learn the forward cast is to allow the line to fall on the ground at the completion of the back cast and then practise from that position. Make sure that the line is straight out on the ground behind you—a good straight back cast is the foundation of a good forward cast.

Photograph 8 shows that the casting arm is fairly low and the left hand holding the line is practically up to the reel. From this position start moving both hands forward at the same time. This is a very important point—many anglers at this stage make the mistake of moving one hand

⑫ ⑬ ⑭ ⑮

much faster than the other and the technique breaks down, so make sure that both hands are kept together and tension is kept on the line with the left hand.

At the start of the forward cast the body weight will be on the right leg, but as the forward cast progresses the body weight will move onto the left leg. Also, as the forward cast progresses, the hips pivot from the right to a square-on po-sition (see Photographs 10 and 11). You will also see from these photographs that the casting arm is starting to move upward and the wrist is well open—this is important because it is the final flick of the wrist nearing completion of the forward cast that helps to impart the high speed to the rod tip essential for distance.

In Photograph 12 you will see that the left hand is about

to haul the line. Full power should be applied just in front of the face. You will also see from this photograph that most of the body weight is on the left leg. These last few body movements will seem fairly slow to begin with but keep concentrating on the correct format and then speed up the movement. At the start of the forward cast, make use of the leg muscles—push off with the bent right leg, quickly pivot the hips to the front and (very important) keep the two hands coming through together. In Photographs 13 and 14 the line has been hauled down the left side of the body. The wrist has also been turned over very quickly at this point. Notice how the left leg has straightened and acted as a brake to the left side.

Photograph 15 shows the follow through with the rod being lowered in order to minimise the friction of the line through the rings—holding the rod tip too high causes a wide angle between rod tip and line, causing a lot more friction and cutting down distance.

The pull in the forward cast, like the pull in the back cast, should coincide with the fastest rod movement, since a pull at the moment of fastest possible tip speed gives the greatest degree of energy to the line. A feeling for the precise moment will come with practice. Often, when practising the forward cast, you hit one just right and away goes the line like a bullet taking all the shooting line. So you take off more line, put it on the ground, and expect the next cast to go even further but it does not happen—probably because you are trying too hard and the correct form has broken down. It is best to stop when this happens, take a rest, and try again. Soon you will find you are getting several long casts in your practice sessions as your confidence builds up.

Once you feel you have mastered both forward and back casts by taking the line from the ground, try the technique with the line completely aerialised. Remember to concentrate on a good back cast, making sure that the line is straight out behind you before starting the forward cast—at all times keeping tension on the line with the left hand.

I found that it paid to spend some time learning distance casting with a double-tapered line, then moving on to monofilament and a short shooting head of around 34 ft. Practise on land until you have the movements mastered before going onto water. Once you are satisfied with your technique you can experiment with longer shooting heads. It also pays to become acquainted with the various weather conditions as different wind speeds require variations in the casting arc for the best results.

These photographs show a long haul down the left side of the body; it is at this stage that difficulty often arises in following up with the left hand. If the haul is made shorter it is easier to control the line. Note also in these two photographs that the head has been turned and the line turnover can be easily followed—this assists greatly in helping to eradicate the second fault of the left hand following the line too quickly.

Two rear-view shots in the distance cast: note the long haul at the start of the back cast and how near the left hand is to the reel at the end of the back cast.

Several difficulties can arise at this stage of the technique and I would like to show how these can be overcome. The first haul during the back cast normally presents three main difficulties. The first, and most common one, is that, after hauling the line with the left hand, many anglers seem to forget about it and hold the line stationary down the left side of the body instead of allowing the left hand to move up towards the butt ring as the line is turning over. The left hand holding the line tight must start to move towards the butt ring as the main line begins to turn over during the back cast. When I was learning the technique and this problem arose, I made a shorter haul with my left hand which resulted in a much easier follow up to the butt ring

with the left hand. Gradually as better control is obtained the haul can be lengthened.

The second common fault is the exact opposite of the first. The left hand is moved up too quickly after the haul is made during the back cast so that instead of waiting until the main portion of line outside the rod tip transmits its tension to the left hand, the angler allows the section of line between his holding hand and butt ring to go slack. The technique has now broken down before it has started since line speed and line control have been lost. Getting into the habit of watching the line as it is turning over in its back cast assists in the co-ordination of the left hand movement.

The fishing situation—high line speed must be maintained throughout.

The third fault is holding the right hand too high at the completion of the back cast instead of keeping the hand low. Holding the rod high on the back cast often results in the line being forced down to the ground too early in the forward cast. For good distance, the rod should start fairly low in the back cast and finish high in the forward cast. To overcome the high hand at the end of the back cast, get into the habit of bending the right leg and putting the body weight on this leg at the completion of the back cast; this will result in lowering the back and right arm. Partial straightening of the right arm to accommodate rod drift helps also.

Hauling the line in the back cast – note the left hand moving towards the right hand, and the position of the feet.

The side cast

You will often find, when fishing stillwaters, that the side cast is very useful, particularly when boat fishing when it helps to keep the rod away from your companion. It is also very useful when fishing in windy conditons, particularly casting along the wind.

To perform the side cast the rod is simply moved from the vertical position to the horizontal position. Practise from this position with only a few yards of line until you have proper control. Soon it will be found that the line can be lengthened and controlled easily.

It is not possible to cast as far with the side cast as the overhead cast since the line is moving only two or three feet above the water. It is easy, however, to reach good fishing distances once the side cast has been mastered. The timing is just the same as in the overhead cast. Always make sure the line is straight in the back cast before starting the forward cast.

When fishing the side cast on reservoirs where there is vegetation, it is a good idea to get into the habit of watching the back cast. By doing this the back cast can more easily be controlled and the line can be cast through openings in the vegetation to obtain a straight line before making the forward cast.

On the forward cast always remember to shoot a little line at the completion of the cast. This gives a much more delicate fly presentation.

The roll cast

There are places in lochs and reservoirs where, because of high dam walls, banking, vegetation or rock formations, it is very difficult (sometimes impossible) to use the overhead single fly cast, since the line cannot be cast to the rear. In these instances it is a great asset to be able to use the roll cast in which the line does not travel behind you. The roll cast must be practised on water and not on grass. The water drag is necessary to create tension in the line, which helps the line loop turn over.

First, get enough line out in order to start the roll cast. This is done by holding the rod butt higher than the rod tip, then by an underhand action—flick the rod backwards and forwards at the same time slipping line out with the free hand until sufficient line is in front of you to cast well.

The next step is to raise the rod slowly until it is just past twelve o'clock and make a smart downward stroke to ten o'clock. The rod should be stopped dead at this point. The line will now roll out in front of you and straighten. The rod should then be brought down to the horizontal position.

To speed up the roll cast and achieve a better fly presentation, hold the section of line between the butt ring and free hand—this will give much greater line speed and control. Shooting line should be done at the completion of power at ten o'clock.

The switch cast

The switch cast is a variation of the roll cast and is useful when there is vegetation both above and behind you. The line is extended as previously described in the roll cast but, instead of the rod being held in a vertical position, it is held in a horizontal position and the line quickly flicked down in the forward power stroke.

Casting in windy conditions

Although many anglers find strong wind a great hindrance, there is no reason not to use techniques which make the wind work for you.

When there is a strong wind behind you, it is necessary to put more power into the back cast to ensure that the line straightens. If the line does not straighten, the flies will often be snapped off when the forward cast is made. Once the line has straightened, the rod should be allowed to drift back to the two o'clock position instead of just after twelve o'clock. Taking the rod further past the vertical will lower the back cast and, when making the forward cast, the line will go out higher. This will make it catch the wind more easily and longer casts with less effort will be possible.

For casting into the wind the converse applies. The strong wind coming towards you will help to straighten the line in the back cast and the rod should be stopped just before twelve o'clock. This will cause the line to fly high on the back cast and on the forward cast it will be low, which is ideal for penetrating the wind. Remember to aim only about one foot above the water when casting into the wind, and to hold the section of line between the butt ring and the left hand tight. This allows for much greater line control and speed and results in a much tighter line loop, which is essential for casting into the wind.

Casting a long line with a strong following wind. (Note the low back cast and the high forward cast.)